# SHEARSMAN
## 103 & 104

### SUMMER 2015

#### EDITOR
#### TONY FRAZER

*Shearsman* magazine is published in the United Kingdom by
Shearsman Books Ltd
50 Westons Hill Drive | Emersons Green | BRISTOL BS16 7DF

*Registered office*: 30-31 St James Place, Mangotsfield, Bristol BS16 9JB
*(this address not for correspondence)*

www. shearsman.com

ISBN 978-1-84861-422-2
ISSN 0260-8049

## Subscriptions and single copies

Current subscriptions—covering two double-issues, with an average length of
108 pages—cost £14 for delivery to U.K. addresses, £17 for the rest of Europe
(including the Republic of Ireland), and £19 for the rest of the world. Longer sub-
scriptions may be had for a pro-rata higher payment. North American customers
will find that buying single copies from online retailers in the U.S.A. will often be
cheaper than subscribing. The reason is that airmail postage rates in the U.K. have
been rising rapidly, whereas copies of the magazine are printed in the U.S.A. to
meet demand from online retailers there, and thus avoid the transatlantic journey.

Back issues from nº 63 onwards (uniform with this issue)—cost £8.50 / $14
through retail outlets. Single copies can be ordered for £8.50, post-free in the U.K.,
direct from the press, through the Shearsman Books online store, or from good
bookstores. Issues of the old pamphlet-style version of the magazine, from
nº 1 to nº 62, may be had for £3 each, direct from the press, where copies are still
available, but contact us for a quote for a full, or partial, run.

## Submissions

*Shearsman* operates a submissions-window system, whereby submissions are only
accepted during the months of March and September, when selections are
made for the October and April issues, respectively. Submissions may be sent
by mail or email, but email attachments—other than PDFs—are not accepted.
We aim to respond within 3 months of the window's closure.

## Acknowledgements

María do Cebreiro's poem in this issue, and those in the previous issue, are taken
from her Galician collection, *Os hemisferios* (Vigo: Editorial Galaxia, 2007),
by permission of Galaxia. The poems by Jacqueline Risset are drawn from *Sept
passages de le vie d'une femme* (Paris: Flammarion, 1985) and are published by
permission of Flammarion. The translations of Esther Jansma's poems in
this issue also appear in *Modern Poetry in Translation*.

# Contents

# Zoë Skoulding

## from *Adda*

### I

a river behind itself
this long s disappearing
seriffed into mud or the
torn edges of a map is

Adda or Adam after
Cae Mab Adda never
an origin only a
dried up rib of a river

a trickle of threat suppressed
escaping the level eye
where sea runs to horizons
innocent as water as

an adder stamped underground
with only the faintest hiss

### II

river subtracted from its
own presence a riverrun
aground secretly working
as all rivers the double
edge of every beginning
u-shaped between its two banks

where flood is defenceless where
water levels the difference

digging the foundations it's
as though no-one remembers
the water the ground is full
of it pumped out only to
rise up through the mud alive


III

flowering at the mouth it
speaks its own name on the point
of losing it becoming
public at a safe distance
our mouths flower in a name
becoming distant to us

what is it you're listening to
there at the lowest point where
the town dips towards what it's
forgotten what's still there on
the tip of the tongue a rush
of kingcup campion bramble

in its stutter is what it's
saying what it's saying is


IV

the camera points at the
faces the river flicks out
of view trout between fingers
gone it was the faces we

5

held in the chemical frame
the soldiers the beautiful
grocer's daughter in shadow
moving through light the city's

dream of itself constructed
on water running under
unspeech in the dank edges
look away now the image
wet at the corners you would
never even glance at it


V


your fluency your vowels
your filth and your contagion
emerge from the mud and rock
becoming the system where
whatever hygienically
comes out of nothing the push
and pull of water under
ground that doesn't speak any
language in its solitude

is water lonely the beach
is a dead end not the way
out or was it ever land-
locked coffers sink and the slate
glitters like all that isn't


VI


doesn't everything run to
the lowest point your cut-price

sables budget peacock silks
flown all the way from China
an hour on the till the price
of a bus fare till the day
ends with all of us in it

river I ask you what's the
point where are you running to
how will you surface is it
only stoppage or sudden
mass that storms the pipes into
these lustre puddles peacock
slicks rising on oiled weather


## VII


what's the difference between a
form and a constraint does one
bottle up the other break
the pattern by showing no
answer only the edges
where does the pressure come from
a crack in the shopfront or
here a spring coiled in a rock
displacement of energy
the shape of water inside
translating itself into
seepage stolen trickledown

that's never enough just some
body's living diverted

# Martyn Crucefix

## The Only Point of Light in the East
*Romania's Great War: abecedaries after Mihail Vladescu*

5. Bathing in the Olt

i.
A modest apartment
a swimsuit which on a famous beach last year in high season had
    caused quite a stir
a well-lit house on a quiet street of the Capital
all part of the performance

an absence that had been longer than expected but through no fault
    of his own
as all miserable people do
as they tried to hide
as you might after a funeral, having stood for hours, the welter of
    powerful emotion
at that very moment Violetta exacting her revenge
aware of his girlfriend's fierce jealousy
Benedict had been adamant
both reproach and bitter disappointment
bringing the conversation skilfully round to bathing
cheat on me – on the very same day you cheat on me – I'll cheat on you

children taking cows to the pasture

close by he saw their naked bodies vanishing among the shadows of
    the willow trees
crushed by the incident, imagining her happiness in ruins, her soul
    flared with the great, heroic decision to take revenge

ii
Dawning on Benedict

deeply

delightful entertainment during the long, hot summer days, bathing
    in the Olt
did not shout
did not threaten, did not say a word
drowning in the whirlpool of the Olt


iii.
Elegant, young, attractive
even Benedict seemed to have lost confidence
forests of osiers, of dense, hollow willow trees and huge sand bars
    that gave the impression of tremendous disturbance
for her these were dreadful moments

given the opportunity to sneak back she swiftly dressed herself
going to bed that night they abandoned themselves to passionate
    embraces
he would not be able to keep the promise he had made when he'd
    left his girlfriend, Violetta
her eternal threat never left his mind
her misfortune was not something Violetta thought greatly about
hidden under the shaggy willow trees on the fine, dry sand, beneath
    the melancholy rays of twilight
his athletic body and complete absence of hair
his body found where the current had brought it to the river bank
his was unexpected


iv.
I am miserable. I am very miserable…
I knew you would want to save me

v.
If it was achieved without much effort on her part
important business would keep Benedict in Craiova for two more days
in contrast she appeared flawless
in his every action he could leave no room for any suspicion
in the carriage on the way they talked little
in vain she pleaded to accompany him

just some beautiful hotel waitress

keenly looking for the dining car waiting to see him
left home alone, spawned a host of suspicions
lovingly aroused by desire, the thought that she belonged to him

Milcoveni to take tea, served according to the rules of a fine house
more than once Mr. and Mrs. Virgil Trancu had been invited to join
    them bathing in the Olt

near the bank the river was quiet
neither love nor life in the old, white house in Milcoveni


vi.
No direct path so they had to make a detour to reach the water
no inkling that anything was amiss
no trace of Benedict
not at all hard to convince. And he surrendered

not taken in by his gesture; it merely fuelled her suspicions
nothing seemed to threaten their happiness
now they had lost almost everything

on the opposite bank something strange was happening
one solitary gesture: one of renunciation
perfectly covering her body it emphasized her beautiful figure
pretending fatigue and weakness

quickly went under without trace

## vii.

Reasons for panic at Milcoveni as the heated imagination of his
    girlfriend
she bent briefly forward as if liable to fall
she had a simple plan
she had made it the night before and she would carry it out
she seemed to be begging for help and attention which she did not need

skirting the strongest currents of the river, he managed to reach the
    other bank
slave to her own impressionable nature, to passionate feelings
so hard to counter. Cautiously, he tried to spare her any pain

so it was that the two couples often met
soil erosion caused by the powerful and frequent flooding of the
    waters of the mighty Olt
some high society woman in Craiova
something of a coward and Benedict a mere beginner
struck out decisively for the side where the current seemed most
    powerful

taken aback and then enchanted by this new music
the "maillots" were brought out and Violetta's was especially fine

the delay seemed to make sense no longer
the fear lovers know when the one they love is not beside them
the grace and elegance of the two girls contrasted sharply with the
    ravines and the river bed, hollowed out by the destructive fury
    of nature

the material evidence . . . He found the two "maillots"


## viii.

The past behind its drawn curtains
the train to Slatina
their loved ones emerged from the glittering water

their property stood on a hill of red soil, a few hundred feet distant
    but facing the river Olt
they were making for the other bank
they'd no thought for the tragedy that had already taken place
this was Violetta now in love with Virgil
though she would have been happy to be rescued

to irresistible longing
to swim where the currents allowed
two nights of absence … to her that was evidence enough

urgent matters would force delay

Violetta seemed to have handled the short separation well enough
Violetta suddenly disappearing from sight
Violetta took her revenge
Violetta was a powerful swimmer

Virgil Trancu and his family lived close by in a neighbouring village
waiting for the scandal to break at any moment
waiting for what he felt sure would happen
warmed sand under leafy osiers in the breath of a day drawing to
    an end

was meant simply to entice him
was out of danger
was wrong and she suddenly burst into tears
yawning, carefully, she un-
zipped her "maillot" and lay indifferently, beautiful and seductive

# Kiran Millwood Hargrave

### chorus cycle: eurydice & orpheus

let's start with the sky    yes the sky    the sky
that  day  was  all  sorts  of  blue  and  pale
set against the forest  where  o  walked and  e
stood root-struck  as a tree  yes a tree  was stuck
on the edge of the forest  where  o  walked
and  e  she waited  though she did not know for
what she had been there so long tied  yes  so long
tied  to that same patch of ground for    so long
laced to that same tight knot of soil    so long
only music played sweet enough to suckle gods  o
only music played like rivers meeting seas    o
only music    could uncoil her toes  and spread
them like lilies  opening out  under full moons
and tip her arms out and    o how o    played
played her in    played her    played her out


played her in    played her    played her out
-side of herself until the world tipped and  off she
flitted  flung like a peach pit  lifted as lightning
through her    l o v e only brings them close as a
letter touch a d o v e flocked  V  land-locked
between  o  and  e  so adored that press tip to
fingertip that meant she had learned  the secret of
flight    and might someday know to fall with
aquiline race  as up his nape she tastes the brackish
taint    late summer blackberries he sang her
sticky and bruise lipped look  e brought him such
song and  he sang her as though she was caught in
his  throat  and  he  sang  her  until  she  was
e  and only and  o  and  always and  o o o
how easy she is shucked from her skin  lifted to him

how easy she is shucked from her skin   lifted to him
as the rainclouds gather    look up    they're filling
gods are swirling the sky    yes the sky    the sky that
we said we would fill and we said would fall the sky will
fill and fall on their heads and o and e are still in bed
learning fingertips    and singing    and seeding
like their bodies are celestial and will not bleed when
bitten    seize when poisoned    rot when dead
when will they learn the shape of things    stop    it
has a fearful momentum they must    stop    it
will not come good in the end no way to stop    it
now monsters are coming    look down    yes down
or even behind    o no    not behind    in hindsight
a backward glance was always going    to end it all
in a backward glance it will all come down    crashing

## Host

Swans have nested
beneath my scalp.
Mornings I feel them
running for take-off,
neat as tadpoles, webbed feet
sticking my cortex. They nibble weeds
from the stem. When they love,
I wear my hair loose and they lift it
from the follicle, pull it in for nests.
When they mate, my nape tingles.
This summer I walk carefully,
my brain full of eggs.

# Simon Perchik

## Four Poems

\*

You try to hide the way all hillsides
are warmed from inside and sunlight
useless, begin each breath

in a mouth far off, lit by thirst
and those slow lips where evenings
come to listen —it's an old sun, one

you're never sure will be a morning
let you surface again, go
as if you were leaving a heart

to give yourself up :a breath
that would empty the Earth —even so
it begins inside a whisper not yet

a mound, with a shadow all its own
spreading out your flowers —a harbor
smelling from distance and spray.


\*

You have a feel for place to place
fresh from the ground and trains
stopping by to check the gates

each station and even in winter
arrives late, surrounded
by a drizzle against the window pane

and your hair can't dry, is trapped
inside this old hat half stone, half
crushed, half its hot-shot tilt

in so many directions at once
falling along the tracks
without a sound covers your forehead

lets it grow old and escape again
is possible without more rain
looking for help or the barracks.


\*

One stone still forming
left to itself though its roots
can't find the place

—from a distance this pebble
is taking so long, sends the others
a signal that is not a morning

not yet rain coming with skies
—it's a dark nothingness, its sparks
still hidden, too soon for the two

that would become a sun
and for the first time
without evenings or the dirt

you grind slowly from footsteps
and loneliness, has the shadow
it needs for rest, kept alive

on the darkness nursing your fingers
pressed against each other and your eyes
without kisses or a mouth.

\*

You lower all doors
the way this knob
works it out where your hold

will slow the sound
waves make starting out
from the sea floor

and your hand stays wet
as if something you said
would fit inside the lips

your heart blows on
that shares its shoreline
between the sea and the shadow

cooling the mouth even seabirds
cover with their wings
their cries and turns.

# Alexandra Sashe

## from *Wandering Cycles*

To restore the outer edge of the table
forced into a faultful square –
to free its initial curve of the circle,
    chisel away the angles
    and save all  without mercy.

The honey voice of the wooden shavings
sings their last, uncovered purpose.
The smooth surface takes over,
along with us, disculpated,
absolved from being
furniture.

        The sunlight bakes us a daily bread
        of nothing – leavened and salted
                with its recurrence.

        The wood shapes our common dwelling
        with its arboreal thought
        and a rings concept.

Walls embrace
our measure of space,
chairs grow backs,
              upright,
attuned with our conscience.

Time and bread cut in slices,
spread with awaiting,
sweetened per serving,
    we eat from the empty porcelain plates.

Metamorphic and static, we slough
our off-white upholstery
and grow skin
    from the warp and weft
of : sunlight, nothing, partaking, tablecloth.

            ( From scripts and plants we collect
            our measure of oxygen. )

We inhabit the centre, the sole room,
its shelves and harbours,
valleys and fields :

            As our armchair
            develops the Ark's capacity,
                we are simplified,
                        perfected,
                            reduced
            to the bare fullness of being.


## Spring Canticle

When the snow subsides
beyond its *raison d'être*,
mills are milling a new flour

the flight of birds,
stripped of its off-white background,
twines with the all-embracing sky
the naked line of the horizon.

the thaw water, pure and delivered,
carries its pearls
of lessness and fullness.
        Orphancy sprouts.   We sit on the porch,
        our eyes welling with sunlight.

## [Untitled]

The renewed kingdom
deserts its gardens.
         It is a small walk,
under the sun
recoiled into its zenith.
The path strews petals
to cover the paving stones'
soteriological configurations.

The obvious kingdom
embraces its source
with counterfeit lips,
counter-kneels, engenders its own accord.

The kingdom's halt is hidden in steps,
imprints of its heraldic mirrors
through which leaks
         at the kingdom's feet
the face it carried on its temples.

# Tim Allen

## 6 poems from *A New Geography of Romanticism*

1.
place the dancer in diluted solution
lose her face in the mathematical shadows
runaway hermit devoted to lute's barometer
turn away turn back once undiscovered

a simple death fall of night old desires
undercover gives you one way out
dissolute yet fizzing with twisted nostalgia
painting a white sail on the burnt black wall

unconscious diamond loathes its lucidity
nitpicky surgeon's self-conscious s/kills
filing clerk scarcely drifts over flaky lake
borderline child initiates the hypochondriacs

2.
maxim thrives in speed-writing antidote
spade's multiple surfaces dig up 9 dimensions
doubtful automaton patrols an avenue of hives
mineral as crude as stereotypical water

plump spermatozoa of well respected recluse
ending a manifesto rather too abruptly
euphonic eunuch repopulates the world
flying fish stranded photo-finish

don't do what I do but do write soon
quantumly spying as if forging hidden gifts
solicitor's tone alone confounds torturer
stranded needles of light on the tin-foil moon

3.
dogma horror quasi-muse proto-disco
3 friends count (on) each other on 4-poster
pair reappear eclipsed on the end of the pier
spherical slippers all kicking off

meaty 4-liners meet their 3 manufacturers
languid invertebrate mercy
we thought you would want to be disturbed
psychosomatic gestation period

gin and orange put on a last second spurt
do-gooder works harder home from home
egging on distressing bride blood
taking a microscope to the country's cobbles

4.
untidy square unrecognizable at rush-hour
comical incendiary device on sentry duty
patient stars experience a randy hush
regrouping around a temporary judgment

"now listen up you rehearsing shapes"
farm further up-field from a parking-up drug tsar
crooked stag pejorative gets suburb in a flap
the cubists are coming to kill us with a car

there's a basic ugliness in this essential grace
underused Mass Observation
fly-past clears a mail path through colliding snails
your soft edges are as hard as hair

5.
mislaid the concept of lunch while looking for art
art material street named after our children
bus arriving late is your final prompt
top deck crowded with transparent children

shelved reactions foretell reference
thank you 'specially for the tranquil repair job
pretending to read a book about avant-garde cinema
telling yourself the time

a right reverend posture picking up a cold-call
electronic librarian's chronic constipation
reach for the high shelf above the book of flames
erratic corners within the carcass

6.
it's gone where nobody can see it or anything
forgotten expenditure forgoes delusion
they planted the stuff in his rabbit backpack
law itself inorganic and unimportant

irreparable ear multiplied by minus 8
an arrogant guilt by association answers—
*not here yet? give it a chance give it eternity mate*
can you make out a language made of light?

to create to celebrate finding content in form
to dream enhanced to drive unconsciously
responsible adult dialogue remote
finds early days essence in a lost adolescence

# sean burn

## cherish the pen, cherish writing, cherish books
*after the film* the colour of pomegranates *(on the poet sayat nova)*
*by sergei paradjanov*

pomegranates bleed
        a slow map
ov the caucasus

        fish out ov water
& a single white rose
        carved in rain
thorns brushing
        childhood

water grooves library walls
the walls bleeding water
the books calling thunder
calling thunder on down

        under tapestries
        the child evades
        the child evading
this—the first site ov exile

the ladder is a knife
the book is a hand
ascend the ladder
        dont stand
on ceremonies
dry out yr reams
        —so many
pages ticking
stand on the spine
play cats cradle

24

mother ov pearl
raining on down

in forbidding love
milks fine lacework
sluices the skin
the poet he is a woman
he is a woman too
brother in blood
sister ov blood
a necklace ov roots
& no-one
no-one rooting
for the poet

the knife is a ladder
the hand is a book
        this freighting
where history presses
                each finger down
each chapter on down
this ever-present load

they marked yu
        w/ sacrifice
        yr wd-be master
blood to forehead
yu cannot rub off
retake yr spiked fiddle
                retake?
retune...

        black seeds
cluster as locusts
the games yu played
the games yu still play
a great unquenchable thirst
encroaching the stonework
ov a latticed mind

           cleave to
cage ov thorns
a cave new-born
feather underlines
a vase   lace is made
its steam intense
occludes the face
veiled gauzy

white eggs in a bowl
& flatbread spread
w/ fine thin soil

& always that tick
                ov books
their pages turning

the white horse
becoming black
the black horse
becoming white
hide yr eyes & ride
                      rings
           around
a single white rose
carved in vain
while ashes storm
           the stairs
& yr horse-backed
poetry performs
a line ov rare fire

the hand stained red
the land stained black
back to back     yu
are him yu are her
children chanting
           now

the whole choir
flooding on in
pickaxe soiled
kneels before
raised pistol
the forts walls
in darkness
                kiss
the peacocks beak
speak into stone
face the sun
the son-she
daughter-he

& the hand stained red
& the land stained black
& above all
                remarkable
clothing afire
two halves
male/female
mirrored
so much lace spilled

again flatbread
wraps soil
snare us
a close star
spar w/
the lone fish
the white rose

window   cave   peacock
punch-drunk on love
        pickaxe digs
the meat hung

charred fragments
ov page blowing
cocoons
the interrogate eye
the writing is pearl
the writing is
w/ pearls
& the spiked fiddle
needs tuning again

lace is spilled
the wall is news
determined
to drink the love
& polish the mirror
the dance ov torso
                exiling yu

tread the grapes
tread the grapes
read the gait
        between
the white horse
& the black
& wait on
the candle guttering
singeing yr name
poet s/he cleaves
spits black seeds
there is no water
s/he slits throats
drinks wine
prepares the meet
whole flagstones
running red
take up the pickaxe
        or the shovel

shovel is good
the soil is oil
poke yr head
thru white lace
sheep released
fill the space
keep shovelling
the oil-black
rock the cradle
rock the cradle
flatbread
torn down
generations

wool broken
on the back
ov wind
until cloth too
becomes ashen

lemons drop
no-one dreams
ov descending
the smaller ladder
screams to undo
invaders / invasion

& flatbread
wrapping soil
is a window
giving out
onto steppe
held in place
by two children
boy-she / girl-he

pomegranates
& blade

both run
freely red
always thirsty
the wine doesnt
touch her/his lips
pours down
her/his chest
pomegranates
full circle
bleed their last

the poet is always thirsty
the ladder is always a knife
the book is always a hand

everywhere horses
change their plumage
plunge forward
always toward
the black horse
but never rein
in the white

a steady stream ov wine

yr spiked fiddle
     detuned
run off land

flatbread spoils
turns the hand

     & everywhere
pomegranates bleed
     a slow map
ov the caucasus

# Michelle Cahill

## Harbour

Because there are no shoals of haddock spawning
he spends the night cutting timber to repair a keel,
gathers faggots in spit rain, in floodwater fields.

The sun's parachute silk settles over chimneys.
Pale clouds hang crowding the sky like driftnets.
Up, up, the black-backed gulls arc into draughts.

A heron hunched on the rocks like an old fisherman
in a raincoat snubs the hushed foray. The tide measures
time as Autumn cobbles the town, deserted by tourists.

Dawn tarnishes roofs, their curved gables, furred
winter trees. Safe from the saltmarsh, the intervallic
hedgerowed fields, he unloads bags of firewood.

He is not the sea's signature, its memory of human
coal, its middle passage of linen, tobacco, gold.
When he is beckoned he leaves the harbour quietly.

The traveller enters the banal to haunt the empty
creels, his seaweed hair. She hears in a pipe rinsing
flagstones, Zambia's swamps—all the drowned past.

# Windscape

A day that belongs to wind, dogs, farmers, colts,
to cranes migrating south in these autumn squalls.
This morning, a lull—for three hours the day was still.

Not completely static for a fieldfare weaved in the holly.
I saw the sprig quiver but failed to notice the mare graze.
The town bustled with pedestrians, tenacious in spirit.

Smell the streets and you are reminded of sludge, coal
rising from underfoot, a rough odour that speaks of toil,
rain, of what feeds us in winter and keeps the town sane.

Hardly do we see the sun. Already it demurs, dark clouds
edge the horizon, the wind throws tantrums, indiscretions.
We are towed by its interior waves, obsessive as dreams.

Try as we may, we can't converse with wind. We can't
ask it to practise restraint. That would be too far-fetched
even for nature. Let the wind soliloquise into silence.

Let it be the tension between us. Today, it translates a
boy's ballooned trousers, a spaniel chasing a flock of gulls,
frayed plastic snagged by trees, an avalanche of leaves.

Just to be outdoors! To watch wind-tossed swallows rip
from private glens to common meadows, shaving the skies.
To hear fences grind, lamp posts screech, the oaks creak.

To be broken or to sing—which is our destiny? A bottle
jangles downhill, leaves scrape, watched by the psychic owl
as the wind's curved reflexion pours into abstract fields.

# Death in Bloomsbury

All day I struggled with the ambiguous weather
as the sun blistered through uncut layers of cloud,
as wind shook the overhanging boughs of plane trees
which had forgotten how to caramelise their leaves.

By dusk I walked along the canal passing barges,
stray cats, cyclists, giant cranes, creels, geraniums,
granaries, lovers kept in sanctuary between locks,
girls in absurd heels holding hands, daisy saplings.

I had been thinking of Jacob Wainwright carrying
half a white man from Africa to Southampton Row
when by coincidence a friend appeared from nursing
her demented Mama. We bundled in the windy street

like dirty laundry, thirsting the future. It hailed swift
as a bullet embedded in the brains of a Syrian foetus,
precise as the quirk of meeting a stranger I once knew,
fatal as a woman being mugged while I drifted home.

I slept in a swoon, tipsy, tranquil, vomiting my words.
The night I was offered the world was the night I died.

# James Byrne

## Improvisations for Adam-Baiting

### I. ROCK

whinnying snakeskin
to the lachrymal girl
fronting the moshpit
who exempts herself
in stretching to touch
the scarred geography
of secondary birth—
water to the sleeping
lifeboat of a ribcage
encases her orphanhood
and the rhino-horned
six-stringed encore is
ejaculatory whenever
he plays the final solo

## II. HEART

bar where dead men
go to die and the dandy
barman stiffs Chuck
another carafe of wine
under the thorn-tether
of his brow and droopy
eyes—for Chuck who
dies piecemeal when
pre-electing men over
women—revelling in
himself made mystical
announcing to the bar
'when I knew women
I knew my own heart'


## III. FIRE

clinkered to fire how is it
women live to the strike
of a matchbox while men
grow more crooked—as if
adam died before he had
time enough to recast man's
beastliness among animals—
fire from a dowry's length
lit by the original mother-
fucker who is matricidal
as the sun burns—like
Coriolanus saving Rome for
one woman—Volumnia—
her hushed cry of fire

## iv. Sex

Eve's newest contortion
refolds her like a paper
dragon (man's nature is
indulgent as breath itself)
gentlemen do not read
gentlemen magazines
yet the broadsheets are
colonially impervious—
Purves' western frippery
as if sex were a fulcrum
of Asia not the cockroot
of my neighbour across
a hallway of glass planted
towards the tv screen


## v. Naked

or as if from skin's tunic
to a lovejoy's messabout
or a walking targetboard
sinisterly franchised in
gold Armani and who in
ipod silence doesn't hear
how she had it coming
or how the Styx is held
open to the bling of heaven—
love cools under the net
that covers her—as if
she might be deeper
than a handful of cloth or
something to be reaped

## VI. BREAD

in the sweat of your face
you shall eat bread means
a fair day's work earns
a fair-floured loaf not
being told to calm down
dear because it's only a
(testosterone) commercial
when the cabinet is full
of men born to rule
who would sweat dry
an entire country and dock
a single-mother's right
to be free from the turd-
baking of errant husbands

## VII. MONEY

Belle de Jour calls it self-
empowerment at three-
hundred pounds an hour
but the shot-silk Burmese
teens treading bath foam
in Patpong might suggest
otherwise (if allowed to
speak at all) curious maybe
at the banking of after-
dinner-speaker rates and
the callgirl's uncontrollable
smile—tithed as they are
to trafficking and the
plow of stag weekends

# Laura Elliott

## the inadvertent surrogacy of matchboxes

Collecting matchboxes bled into an enquiry
of locations. Connect the matchbox
in the pinetum with the shattered birdcage,
the matchbox on the mountain path
with the hot spring, or the appearance
of the hot spring on the mountainside
silence. And now connect the matchbox
to the river's green frosted glass
your body brings in to the guest room,
the blue that lingers around your outline
in an unmixed pointillism. There was *bharat gold*
in the valley, *deluxe bhola* and *chameli*,
a green feathered weed. At 32.2666700/
77.1666700 short-sights clapped on a waterfall
washing down a Himalayan slope
to a holy spring in a ancient village,
the light dimmed, disanimated,
and our not hearing it not feeling it –
like the mute red *lal mirchi*, cardboard super roshni
swept off the balcony – was stunning.
Would you describe the chakor as ulular,
would you say that it howled
through the phalanx of trees
when the stripped trunk crashed through
the roof of the aviary? We will call her *Jodi.jpeg*
*19 of 39*, yellow winged beneath the mushroom stalks
on the matchbox we retrieved,
scanned onto *indianlitter.tumblr.com*,
beside fragrant *jeevan, image/62060215943*.

# Conservation

In the lecture on Japanese paper
I learn not to overcompensate.
In the lecture on delaminated
leather board corners I learn to lead
the hog hair deep within. In the lecture
on mechanical damage I learn
that to understand the tear you must
understand the bevel. The wing of
the stealth bomber was designed as a result
of such understandings of the diffused
edge of paper, undetectable as
this wheat-starch-paste patch and just as simple.
Chemically stable, crisp diagonal,
there is a well-known phrase in these circles
which transliterates as *waste can be*
*valuable.* A fracture at the centre
of a leaf can be caused by stresses
in the future. In the lecture on lime-
cured-parchment-dried-under-tension I learn
I too want to shrink under less than
ideal conditions. In the lecture
on Static Grade 100 Micron I learn
*mini baking parchment roll from Lakeland*
*is ideal.* The Northrop Grumman B-2
Spirit has a wingspan of 52m.
Tug the tissue outwards from the contour
to form a hairy fringe and integrate
the fibres. This is an innocuous
binding and is completely reversible.
This is an aeroplane which is invisible.

# James Bell

## rutabaga in a landscape

ectopic engineering schools have become schools
omnium medical schools have become schools
passionate schools have become schools of finite
older schools and never been schools have
become grounded in a science of design fraud
a list of food is provided:
rutabaga should not be eaten more than once a week
among philosophers of science nobody wants
there is a rebirth of interest in the ancient topics
we cannot say what it is/ that we know
in our pattern of action/ our feel for the stuff
ordinary people often think about what they are doing
this entire process of reflection is central to the art
there is nothing strange about the idea


## Kinryusan Temple in Asakusa

*after Hiroshige*

begin with a word for snow

happenstance says the turn of a page
       will reveal somewhere familiar
              forgotten until returned to now

takes the word away
       and settles for snow as it falls
              beyond the paper lantern held
                 up with rope from below

although large it cannot dominate
    in the asymmetric shift to the left
to bring in the red and green of the entrance gate

both croppings are the frame we look through
    as if this is a film still and will
        unfreeze then move to show me more
and this is really a temple we visited

snow is only frozen water

there are no footprints though people walk
    either side beside snow filled trees
        and buildings across a vast expanse
of white that recedes in a reversed V
        to display an early use of perspective

people as pins of colour under parasols
    walk towards the flat red
    of the temple's shapes
        walk as if the ground is white paper

far from cicada song in summer
    when parasols are for shelter from the sun

when people seem still to walk towards
    instead of from the temple

though the scene has a silence associated with winter
    angles fixed and nothing moves

end with a word for snow

## above Kerstéphan

the stones
do not surprise
always now bulk
poised on hilltops
like a giant builder's desertions
scrape the sky
when mist links it to the ground
in a soft vice

threaten to push a round boulder one day
to see if it will dislodge
though none have been moved in centuries
by winter gales or cracked in sun
while soil was sifted from them with
wind or water or both
carved shape from the granite
into an exhibition
cattle ignore
hunger only for hay or wild grass
and nettle
that along with gorse
would soon close the show
glimpsed for seconds on tight bends

deference is an alien idea
each element will not allow
is a seed swept away for lack of dirt
even this far inland there is salt
tasted in wet air from the Atlantic
its mineral flenses memories into unusual forms

# Michael Farrell

## Order

'The sacred is order'
Like pyramids; Akhenaten's cult

Settlement is an order

Oodgeroo's editor made her Bora Ring
(The shape of her Bora Ring story)
A rectangle

Her Rainbow Snake a rectangle

Make of that (a rectangle snake)
What you will

Reading the Aboriginal petitions of the 1920s-30s
The letters to newspapers
(1940s, 60s)
I'm struck by the theme of friendship
The black hand offered to the white

This is the clasp on the cover
Of Robert Walker's *Up Not Down Mate*
(The first edition; the second portrays an Aboriginal flag
And a hand against prison bars)

Walker yelled a lot his last night

Settlement and Federation and mapping
The coastline

Feeding the young man
That escaped from gaol on his birthday
He was already wearing a crucifix

To reverse Stevens: humans are earth
(Soil stone sand and sea)
They're not walking maps
From above they are points
(Pyramid points become blobs)
Numbers of people make blobs too
And sometimes rings, snakes

Hymns are of an old, Greek order
(Relatively old)

The poems of Kevin Gilbert are not like hymns
If anything they protest the loss of hymning

At least it seems that way to me

In the 'Native Settlements' like Moore River
(Featured in the film *Rabbit-Proof Fence*)
Young Aboriginal students read the Bible
(Just as they do in juvenile detention now)

At times they were allowed into the bush
And learned from the elders
This apparent contradiction allowed an extension
Of control
As did trivial permissions and underfeeding

The effect of the Stolen Generations is not only
One of history, the story of Gladys Gilligan
For example
Late of Moore River Native Settlement

When I read the language of Aboriginal friends
On Facebook, I see the influence of African America
A marker that they 'own'

Just as Christianity differentiates country people
From the faithless urban 'arm'

It's not just Cook that makes this poem possible
But the Wurundjeri Council
Their office at Abbotsford Convent
A short bike ride away
From where I write this in my prism
(Seen as a rectangle from above)

Yet I remember the earthquake when
This building moved (relatively) like a snake

# Keri Finlayson

## The wren, that gossip, is a fine one to talk

small girl:  From Flushing Falmouth rose up like a wave.
I rode the jogging foot plate of the pram
along the muddy tow path as it broadened
into street then hardened at the very end
as cottages.

> *the wren (singing) :*  *Listen to the women tell themselves worlds*
> *Chanting it all as the lives unfurl*
> *Listen to the women tell themselves worlds*

small girl:  I saw two-up, two-downed rows of false
and distant aunts.
They gathered in the smeechy back
to trill tight shapes, rocking themselves joyful
with spite and the shared electricity
of unkind words.

> *the wren (singing) :*  *Listen to the women tell themselves worlds*
> *Tonguing and glossing each kink and curl*
> *Listen to the women tell themselves worlds*

small girl:  These powerless, powerful,
nylon pinnied school friends of my Nan
clotted the world with their making breath.
Tattled up ghosts, the sins of their fathers
making flesh from rough words.

> *the wren (singing):*  *Listen to the women tell themselves worlds*
> *Chanting it all as the lives unfurl*
> *Tonguing and glossing each kink and curl*
> *Listen to the women tell themselves worlds*

small girl:    Those were false and distant villages
    sung to life.
    Inconstant.
    Vagrant
    Animated by animosity.
    Wren, they were no better than they ought to be.

# Tania Hershman

## Conversation With a Taxi Driver

Mirabella's mast, the world's largest, he tells me, holds inside its vastness: stairs. No more scaling rigging, a civilized ascent. Mirabella's mast, he tells me, is made of lead, and we don't know, he says, why it is so tall. Just because it can be. A son, he tells me, drives around a General, he's an army man. David, he says, David is treated well. I imagine, as we drive, the son, inside Mirabella's mast, leading his General by the hand. Where is my command? the old man says. Here, whispers David.

## Bridal

Today it only took a garment bag
to make me feel inadequate it
hung from the strap of her rucksack in front
of me in the queue one word BIGGER than
the rest of course it held the dress and god
forbid it should be packed no
she must carry it like a child so
all of us wedded or not will know

# Sarah James

## Purple

His name is not William;
the wheelbarrow we haven't got
is not red and the ungreen bottle
is not broken, but down to the last
heavy scent of lavender.

A filmic gloss. Our bath
gleams empty cream. Void
of violets, the first crocus
splitting winter, juice of true
cherries and bramble wine.

No memories of Magenta
driving him ins-a-a-a-a-a-ane,
Amsterdam smoke inhaled,
snakes uncoiled in his veins,
their ps-t hiss hazed. No.

My apology's shrugged.
Stress eddies his brow, throws
claw lines. I offer a kiss
and the last plum from the table.
He doesn't bite; leaves its amber

whole, next to the bottle –
its shape emptied of foam
but bubbling with resonances,
upon which so much depends
while water still pours,

while the hospital where we met
still has wings and white walls,
while corridors are endless,
purple with dried blood
and long night calls.

"Remember when…" I start.
At last, his lips arc red to a smile.

# A Peacock's Eye

Se faz favor,
      the peacock's ruffling
            stance proclaims.
      His feathers' span
fills the camera lens
      – zoom, then pan –
            ends curling out of frame,
      as he turns tail,
bending from blues and greens
      to a pale shell of spines:
            beauty's ribbed cage.
Beyond his vision.
Not so vanity's claw-grip,
      its arced peck.
            Disturbed dust curves awe,
      undewed at our feet.
Our host, Senhor Sousa,
      flourishes garnished lobster
            to a champagne couple.
We crack open smaller shellfish,
suck up the sea's crusts,
      presented from behind
            the fanned serviettes
      gracing our table.
Pink spark of shrimps.
      Open-winged mussels.
            Black gooseneck barnacles:
      opal-mosaicked,
life's fragments
      shining obrigados,
            shark-tooth sharp.


se faz favor – 'please' in Portuguese.
obrigados – 'thank you' in Portuguese.

# Simon Smith

## from *ZEROFOURZEROFIVEZEROSIXTWENTYTWELVE*

### International Date Line

La Jolla fog-bound looking over the cliff
to 30 or 40 cormorants bobbing up
& down Pacific surf
behind the wheel of the Accent GL, 12.49pm
north on I-5 miss
the turn for I-405, so carry
on the I-5, across east
to west on I-22 to meet the 405 again
drop away to Manchester
Avenue et voilà the door to Guy and Béatrice's, 8128 Airlane Avenue
    3.47pm
check the hire car's over-active air con. Check.
Talk & beer, cheese, fresh pineapple, more talk LAX
on time. Check-in on time. Departure to Heathrow. On time.
Taxi 3.16 pm London, 7.16 am LA.
copies of *OR* Issue Eight line my suitcase
'Ode: Sat Nav Narrative on Flying into LAX'
'Los Angeles River'
'Eyewitness News'
'Paradise Cove'
    —   included
a full run (1-8) for the Poetry Library, London


### Two Days Old

two days ago
this was the lo-fi solution
choose the right
book for my flight (Blackburn's *Proensa*? Guy's *Last Words*)—it's the
    grief

of ending
the journey I feel
the grief                    sipping Mongoose still @ 38,000 ft in the
    Surma, Dulwich
a TV chef's endorsement beams away from the wall
comfort food for missing
a wife                    this-day-of-our-Lord
twenty-second-of-April-two-thousand-&-twelve
imagining as far west as the west will be imagined
                            for sir's palate
a little heavy red
                oh, its oh two forty-two am in London
the evening has just begun my body sez


## Rehearsal

start late: 11.30, Sam's place
Matt set up, David
arrives with his poem, me with mine
'Constellation'
            Evan later
new tenor, with a passing acquaintance
record         sample         rehearse         re-record
'Constellation'
chaffinch & gull                    chirrup & cry
snuck in their chat


                            @4.30
a two hour drive to Essex, *Miles in the Sky*, then migraine on the
    twenty-five no
focus to the left
eye
peripheral                cocktail of lack
of sleep & jet-lag
                driving

my mother's neatly cut two rounds of sandwiches
cheese & pickle                    eyesight
back, memories to school                    packed lunch, the squares neat
folded into grey
grease-proof paper                    times
ten years into how many


                                   lemon-sole, one
Sauvignon, one Chardonnay & chat for now                    Burt
Bacharach, on BBC 4, 'the look of love,' nineteen-sixty-
eight lives forever


## Ode in the Shape of a Lament

'Early Signs Point to Second Term for Tory'—so four more years of
     Boris then—
fitting to a less than perfect twenty-four hours—ten years
since Keith's death—Dorothy in a terrible state—David's
now diagnosed diabetes—the phone line down—the Internet
down—no Skype for days—all in sympathy like a drooping flag
or colour—you 6,000 miles adrift, Miles
Davis' 'In A Silent Way/It's About That Time,' the only
consolation, & dreaming of Catullus
I return to Brandon Brown & the Zukofskys'
catch the 6.38 from Canterbury West not knowing
what we'll eat flying thru grey
dusk the Kent countryside translated into London Bridge

# Rupert M Loydell

## 'A Process of Discovery'
*for David Miller*

'My writing must also, along
what unfamiliar way,
be company?'
  – David Miller, 'Unity'

The poet's book is one of the four I have brought away on holiday. It was a choice between my favourite versions of the short narrative poems of a Greek author, made especially awkward by the translator, who does not appear to be fluent in English, and my friend's new book.

Eventually, I decided on the poet's new collected poems, and looked forward to the dislocation between warm Tuscan light and the nameless grey cities that often form a background to his fragmented texts.

With shutters pinned back, windows wide, sun burning through morning cloud, the poems speak of love, confusion, moments and ideas, all threaded into necklaces of language.

•

The colours in my set of paints never match the colours outside. I have to work hard to find the muted tones of mist or dusk, even more to mix the faded earths and stones, the burnt greens that fill the view.

I have little need for red – a few roof tiles here and there, and only use yellow to mix variations of foliage in the distance. Neither the earth not stone seem at all brown, more grey and off-white. The distant mountains require blue to give them distance, purples and greys if the light has gone or a storm arrived.

•

There is hardly any music here.

Sometimes a faint radio
in the distance,
a few CDs in our hire car
for long journeys,

those drummers we watched
at a medieval fair –
the whole village play acting
for a weekend.

A falcon flew
off into the silence.
A saxophone,
a clarinet:

reported
conversations
on the pages
of his book.

•

Despite itself,
the silence
is the event,

the appearance
of the angel
is the event,

the moment
as pregnant
as the madonna;

bird spirit
of God
top right,

a sparrow
flying across
window-framed sky.

•

In one version the angel
speaks in painted script,

is always speaking,
never silent.

I prefer the mute
gold wings of flight,

the ethereal earth
beneath celestial feet,

the always unsaid
unbelievable truth.

•

The poet's book has served me well, and has sat literally and
conceptually alongside a short book on colour, a re-read novel of
occult training and enlightenment, and a fictional exploration of
moments when the celestial and human met or even touched.

Our conversation has been a long one. We first met on the page and
later in the flesh, but there is still a lot to be said.

For the moment, I am again listening.

•

The sun is even brighter now.

It is clear my painting's colours are all wrong.

I rinse my brushes and head out for a swim.

A startled lizard runs from the sudden splash.

NOTES

The title is a quote from David Miller.

The Greek author was Yannis Ritsos.

The four books were David Batchelor's *The Luminous and the Grey*, Jim Dodge's *Stone Junction*, Karl O. Knausgaard's *A Time to Every Purpose Under Heaven* and David Miller's *Reassembling Still – Collected Poems*.

# James McLaughlin

## Age

Under ashen grey skies
an
unvariegated screech

credulous I
the heron gullible
and domicile

one foot
on a rock
tenuous/ liable

it is there precipitous
as I
or Gods
or memories
die

## if

The wind today in the long grass
sways and drifts to my nostrils.
Flies flick from the moss - its
noble so to be fauna: the air is
succulent as the sand
that twist in the bay.
The gulls have no intention
of dying—every
tree convulses with memory.
Each leaf and thorn forms a denial.
Gesture, sun, colour, breeze, texture, nuance,  air,
intersperse, overlap, hinge
on this moment.

Now possibility exists / becomes
mountainous. I may die
in such possibility?


## As is

a construed actuality to a
narrowing to saudade or
a variegated wisp a
vine  a vague
propulsion forward to a

preposterous yearning
a
(flight of tension)
or osculating  twist  / after
rainbows  retrench too clear
worming purple and
and

windfall apples darken in
the wind / hint tone
blemishing  pockmarks a
scratched trauma
bits of
scabs, things mutilate too some

mirth and mayhem
alternately appear
on every other constituent
and a
disfigurement wounds
on the littlest of things on
the tiniest of things

# Kate Miller

## Reach

*Peignons comme chante l'oiseau*   *Claude Monet*

A cry stiffens the pool's skin. Thin slip of wind
puts on a little flesh, stirs the stream.

I'm keeping one eye on the boat while Blanche sets out my paints.
 We lumber from the mud and dead reed dip of riverbank.

   Blow, wind, cheers a bird, shake the stream awake,
     show her your violet streak!

Send her down the river, to rinse in the breath-warmth of creatures,
vole-squeak, cow-sigh, scratch of a heron shifting heddle feet.

A branch, then an eddy flips glass hair of willow.
 Water holds a smeary mirror up to tips of light.

    My other eye is climbing into space to reach
by stairs of cold, spires topping the air's cliffs of ice.

As birdsong rises, as water winds, is winched upwards
 in the screw of poplars, as vapour lifting to a clearing sky

is gathered in the net, we mark each break in the mesh of morning
  mended with wires of light.

# A bird does not sing because it has an answer

*from the Chinese proverb*

Sylvie has stayed out all night for weeks in search of roosts.
Alert to early jostlings, on her haunches in a beechwood
she's matching *teek-a-teek-a*
                              *fu phew fu yeeu-yeeu*

        in electronic shorthand. Technically
a whizz, she's been inventing
ring-tones on a cell-phone since the nineties.

That's not the hard bit; now to perfect an app
to locate the territorial—and arboreal—zones each cockbird claims
to own, starting calling before dawn.

She has translated *tik-at, tsi-tsi-tsi,*
*tikat tsi tikat tsi-tsi* but she's stuck on *a-wah awa .. awa*
*hoo,          who?*          spacy and euphonious,


                        the sudden brash alarm of *TSEEP*
*TSEEP* and a sneezing *TSEUT*
        followed by a little *tseep*, then the hurried *uppa  uppa, uppa*
*pew*, which keeps Sylvie on her toes; she wants to factor in
breath taking and the pause,
                            the pause      the pause
for sunrise, the falling mute, a little shuffling on the twigs
            (the trees put on their gloves of light)
Sylvie gilded, head cocked birdlike, waiting for the first
hen to break her silence.

# John Phillips

## Shape

It's not that I
presume you are

here listening
just because I

am here speaking.
That's not it.

Perhaps no
one is here.

There are words,
or such is

apparent. But words
do not mean

someone is saying them
or someone is

listening. Anymore
than a chair means

someone must be
present to sit

in it, or even that
it was made

for the purpose
of sitting.

## Gratitude
*for Fadhila Chabbi*

Wherever I walked dust covered my tracks

Whatever I made fell into a thousand pieces

Whatever I said was lost in the wind

Whoever I loved loved nothing in the end

Whoever I created vanished the same


## Meaning

It's not to
say anything

but to think
some thing

not thought
before it

is said
makes this

what
it is

# Andrew Taylor

## Passing Place

Stonechats dart before the prow
down five miles of single track

ten year atlas
                    fifty year old map

John Bartholomew & Son Ltd Duncan St Edinburgh

Along the burn a diversion
slow flow              fast flow

Mary's Bridge  becalmed
stone gathered clear pool

shaped like the original
pool of home


## Mending Kit

Enter sit

a line written in the shelter
square marked territory

And gaze

And gaze

leaves gathered framed
straw lined diagonal

at the sky

at the sky

Open
summer until 17.00
winter until 16.00

## Scottish Blend

Like the plain it is probably
the water

airport lights five miles away
seem closer

green signal allows for movement
along the coast

Work to an early morning deadline
sleeping bag sleep

walk to the station
to take a five pound shower

before resumption
the rain brings out the swallows

# Geraldine Clarkson

## Lustre

I've raggled my tail thinking of her. Gross glister of skin
above drooped stockings. Eyes pissed, her twitching
stick neck. Her caked face all lacework and doughy pasta.
I'm maddened with why he wants her lumpen lustre
when I'm clean and neat as a tine and faster
than him or her and can more than pass muster
in and out in the mornings before they're awake, the master
first and her the last, dreamless till noon, mouldy sister, I've cussed her,
swallow blades when I think how he's kissed her, how he says like a
    ninny
he's missed her when she's away, won't know himself for joy when—
    *basta!*—
he's lost her. By my kind grace.

## When my enemy came home with my love,

                     I was on the
phone. Necking-and-chinning my mobile, I chased them into the
kitchen. My love ended up in the corner. My enemy between us.
Glowing. *Don't give me a bloody hug, then*, I made a kind of lunge,
uncharacteristic. The glow baffled a bit, knocked to one side, then
the other—*puff!*...*puff!*— the way white flour in a clear polythene
bag might do if punched. We went back into the main room and
she folded languorous limbs against a lovely long blue body while
she recounted the wonderful afternoon they'd had. I heard about a
wonderful meal at a place called *Santa Lucia*. *Sahn-tah Loo-CHEE-
ah*. A laugh. Delicious giggles like the longest glasses of cool Orvieto
wine. In a low voice some trembling revelations she'd been party
to, hinted at. Flashes of glow. Here and there. Everywhere. A glass
shatters. Chaos.

# Mother's Rue

*If only she'd loved enough – Marlon Brando*

What is petersham? What are fearnought, flock, sassafras and percale? The oil from crushed seed of Marlon, the witty helps and artly disposing of beds; the increase of the moon; the goodness of the earth, verbal shadowboxing; kinds of dung. I circle around and around. Focus on me. Don't you think you should go to sleep? I don't always feel the same way. Once I was in a play. I tried so hard. Laudanum is an anaesthetic. From what is it obtained? What is felt? Bud, the plump, holding onto me, like a piece of porcelain. It has to be 1 pm. The piercing of our mother who ran away from home every Sunday. The lantern slides. Flatter. Watch her breaking apart.


# Alacria

Did Alacria survive her upbringing in the state of
despair? Did she hone her bones with fasts and
stretches till they looked like they belonged
to an Egyptian princess? Did she feel more like a
Phoenician? Did she carry on counting days till
she could see her father in Indian gold summers
and did he cradle, cradle? Did she stuff everything
which mattered to her ? Did she say no
to every man who proposed
an escape? Certain
her father would come back and that when he did
he would lift and cradle, lift and cradle, lift and
ease/ drift/ tease?
Did she write in hieroglyphs?
Did she get involved in pyramid
sales? Did she hardline the women? Did she henna
her hair to match the beeches in the oldest
garden, the one where she was three? Did she go for

the moon and minelight? Did she avoid
pickets and pickpockets, husbandpickers
and picnics? Did she over
subscribe to harebrained schemes,
over and over? Always with a nubby hope that the next
manilla letter would hold an encrypted
plea? A sign, signed? And then would the moon
draw tides in a circle, and her blood shoot up and stop
dragging? And would there be water for the urchin children
with their parched smokers' voices? Who kept asking her to do more
favours? Who kept pulling at her skirts and saying 'just this, just this'?

# Zoë Skoulding & Robert Sheppard

## from *EUOIA: European Union of Imaginary Authors*

### Cyprus Gurkan Arnavut (1978-)

### Not Just the Suitors

Not just the Suitors. Their lovers too the bad maids
strung up along a cable {epic simile} like birds caught
in a net in a thicket till their legs stopped wombs
dropped. Like civilisation my compatriot Aphrodite
born from a cut. We're still on the line where the page
thickens towards forgetting / a starfish city split
by spilt foam washes at the edges. When carrying
this graft of atrocity and other aphrodisiacs
we're aphotic with despair aphonous with grief
a writhing tongue lashing ourselves to the mast
listening to keel's creak / wheel's squeak / sail's frap
and swooning in the void where the voices should be.
Pop songs from minarets: the channel switches mid-
current in saturated waves {braced notes} the call
to prayer never so loud as in its tuning out. Whose
love comes through the cables / in what frequencies
on the wave spectrum jostling for decibel-music / with
what frequency do trim voices bleed into prime time?
Do they scissor 'the price of the Euro decision for the
{celestial static} haircut of Greek debt'? No doubt
the other walks beside me and the other's other
slices through the shadows / each step cutting through
the space between heartbeats / in constant deficit {love
owed}. No ownership is not barbaric / no love not debt /
no cable of yellow electric bulbs stretched across the carnival
not darkened by smoke haze. Dimmed in hermaphroditic
indifference desire dissolved in equity the other becomes

the same in toxic exchanges of war graves {peace claims}.
From hand to hand my trembling right becomes tangential
to the act. Who am I if not this beginning on a table where
different worlds come into view / do-it-yourself death mask
beyond the glass of tea / not in the room but part of it.
Half of me slips from the stool. The poem shatters
and its worlds flatten on the fifth wall of space / time
demands she drops a headscarf leaving the table / its moment
won't return though she will to find it neatly folded
{double surface}. In the soft threads of another life
we cover and uncover the details that will never hold
together / each one unravelling its own past. Yes / this
means you. Or the cat wandering into no-man's land
sinewy with insinuation her soft pads assimilating
human ground. Hot towel on your face at the barbers / you
hear the sharpening of cut blades and hope your muffled
defence 'I am not Stavros Monopolous' will save you.


## While Egrets Rise

While egrets rise under my eyelids
and the clock needles its way
into morning, it's as if weather
is all I've ever lived. When history
is a flip of last year's calendar
doing service again as a ladder
up this year's spine I cringe
before diurnal crests unctuous foam.
While every hour is water incessantly
returning every spring a loosening of
pins that hold the joints in place where
the tide turns on every bristle of my
wings tense against lover or prey
neck twisted like toilet plumbing the blaze

of scissored beak and beaded eye glides
to lock my claws around the bough for waiting.
Inland the dry ground turns in on itself
to warbler and wheatear the hoopoe's
spread wing. In time every song finds
its own way through the cracked air
to the cracked ear, even the hoopoe's,
triplets of dull barbs tracking on a green
string across a screen, 23 seconds
of filtered white noise behind which
wings rustle with the soft rush of
disappearing cash. Change is no change
at all shriek the birds disappearing into
money into the sky's indivisible walls.

# Virgil

## translated by David Hadbawnik

### *from* The Aeneid, Book VI — Visit to Hell

*[On their way to Italy, the Trojans make a detour to hell to consult the ghost of Aeneas' father. With Palinurus the pilot having fallen over the side and drowned, Aeneas steers the ship.]*

1. *et rabie fera corda tument*

Thus bawling Aeneas
      guides the fleet to Cumae
      they drop anchor and eagerly
      young men flock the shore
           some seek flame-colored
      sparks in veins of flint
           others scour
      the hills for game

But pious Aeneas heads for the high citadel
where Apollo rules and beyond that
      the sanctuary of the dread Sibyl
a huge cave into which the god breathes
      whiffs of the future

Daedalus      the legend goes
      fleeing the realm of Minos
landed here on his homemade wings
      and dedicated this place to you
           Apollo, stowing his flying machine
           in the giant temple

On the gates it shows the grisly death
      of Androgeos—below that, the punishment meted out
      to Athenians (poor bastards!)

who had to hand over seven newborn sons
        each year for a cruel lottery

On the opposite door
        another horrid scene—
the bizarre love of Pasiphae for a bull
        and the horned progeny
of mixed race—crime's keepsake
        the Minotaur
        and that infamous house
        of unsolvable error
—which Daedalus managed to unravel for the sake of
        Ariadne's great love
        guiding Theseus' blind steps with a thread

You, too, Icarus
        would've been part of the tableau
had grief not stopped your dad's hands

So the Trojans stare at the gates until
Achates brings back the priestess who says

        "Snap out of it—
        right now you'd be better off
        slaughtering seven bulls
        and so many sheep
        as custom demands."

Aeneas does as he's told.
        The priestess calls to
        the Trojans
and through the hundred holes
        of the huge cave voices rush
        to answer her—
The truthseekers come to the doorway
        and she says
                "It's time
        to seek the oracles—
        god behold god."

And she freaks out

       face            explodes

           hair              wild

      breast        heaves

           rage          soul

               giant          inhuman

                    woman

      swelled by       god-breath

she roars

           "WHAT ARE YOU WAITING FOR
                     AENEAS?

        Do you need a fucking invitation
               to fall on your knees
               in prayer?
        Well?    These doors won't open
               themselves."

The chilly silence shudders
        down the prince's spine, and he pours
        out prayers from deep in his chest
             trembling

the Vates still twisting
        under the will
        of Apollo

rages in the cave
        trying in vain to shake
             the god, but

the more she struggles the more
            he takes control—her words
            scream out through
            the hundred cave-mouths:

            "You guys who've endured so many
            dangers (and have more
            yet to come) don't worry
            you'll make it after all—but
            you'll wish to hell you hadn't

                        war      I see
                                        Tiber
            blood    you won't miss
                            the gore
            of Troy                      you'll find
                    another Achilles
            also born                    of goddess
                        Juno    won't be far

            and piss-poor    you'll have to go
                    begging
            in every Italian town
                    you'll wed        an enemy
            lay her down in
                    a foreign bridal chamber
            but keep the faith        brave guy
                    when you least expect it
            salvation comes by way of
                            the Greeks."

Then Apollo pulls back the spurs
            from her heart
                    the frenzy
            stops

## 2. *insano juvat indulgere labori*

"I've heard it all before"
    says Aeneas
    "no new trouble rises
    to meet me, it's all been mapped out

    one thing, though—I need to get into hell
    where my father promised
    to meet me—can you tell me how?"

The Vates responds
    "Blood of a goddess, the doors to hell
    are always open, but finding your way
    back to the land of the living, that's
    the trouble.    Only those Jove loves
    or whose *virtu* lifts them to the stars
    make it back

    But if you're so hot to cross
    the Stygian marsh twice, twice
    glimpse dark Hell
    and indulge in this crazy scheme
        do this first:
    go deep into the gloom of the grove
    and find the Golden Bough
    sacred to Juno—snap off a branch
    for lovely Proserpina who demands
        such offering

    If you're fated to find it
    luck will lead you there, otherwise
    no strength or sharp blade
    will tear it loose.    Also:

    You've got a pal who
    unbeknownst to you
    lies dead and unburied

defiling the whole fleet
while you loiter in our
doorway—go and sacrifice
two black sheep as a down-payment
on expiation. Thus living
you'll see Styx and cross
this trackless realm."

This news hits Aeneas hard.

He and Achates stalk back
to the ships, seriously
                    bummed.

They try to guess who it might be
                    and come upon
the body of
                    MISENUS
          the horn player
who'd fallen to his death
on the thirsty shore

he'd made the fatal mistake
of letting his talent go to his head
playing a tune on
          an empty shell
challenging Triton
to a contest—so the god
caught him and dashed him
down on the rocks

Trojans quickly throw together
his funeral rites

swarming the old woods to cut pines
          axe-blows resounding on oak
          ash-beams going for
          blocks of seats, they roll
          logs down the hills

Aeneas
      musing as they go
      gazing up at the sky      spies two

      DOVES

      recognizing his mother's birds
      his spirits are raised

      "Be guides, you two, I'll follow
      your course through the air to
         the Golden Bough."

They flit through the clear sky
      leading Aeneas down
the stinking hell-mouth, lighting
      atop a tree whence gold
      shines from the branches
Aeneas greedily snaps off
      a glittering twig
      while back on shore the men mourn
      Misenus

paying his thankless ashes last rites

building a huge pyre of rich pine
and oak      whose sides
they interweave with      dark leaves
      adorn it all with gleaming arms
      one group
brings the body forth      hot water seething
      in a kettle and wash and anoint it
         wailing
while others
         go below the huge bier
      to raise the body and solemnly
      torch it

                    Aeneas
himself builds a massive barrow
and puts his friend's things
            his oar and his trumpet
                        inside
so that
            through the ages
            the lofty hill
            still bears the name        Misenus


3. *Procul O, procul este, profani*

There's a great cavern
protected by a foul marsh
where no birds sing—none
could survive the black breath
that spews out over it
which is why the Greeks
call it "Avernus"

                    Here the Vates pours   wine over      the brows
                    of four black bulls     burning     their forelocks
                    calls on HECATE          power    in hell and air
                    others catch hot      blood      from cut throats
                    in bowls  AENEAS uses his own sword to  smite
                    a lamb for Nox and Tellus daughters of  Chaos
                    then slays a barren cow for Proserpina spreading
                    entrails    on flames   at first light    the grove
                    ROARS   beneath their feet slopes move hounds
                    wail   the goddess  approaches  STAND BACK
                    you unholy bastards        the Vates      shouts

"not you Aeneas"
            she continues
            "hold high your sword
            and walk this way—right now
            you need to man up like
            never before"

and she
flings herself recklessly
into the cave, Aeneas
right behind her.

[GODS
who hold sway
over spirits and shades
in all night's wild places
give me strength to sing
what comes next—let your light
shine through in truth
disclosed]


They walk alone through the homes of Dis
picking their way in
dubious moonlight
to the throat of hell
guided by Grief
Disease
Fear
Hunger
oh yeah
and
Death
Hardship
Sleep    and    Pleasure
in    evil deeds
War    Furies
Strife
there are

Centaurs
two-faced
Scyllae
hundred-armed

                Briarus                      monster
                     of Lerna       and         Chimaera
                     Gorgons and Harpies and
                                AENEAS

shakes in his boots his sword      slips in his hand
in sudden fright        if the priestess hadn't warned him
these shapes have no bodies he would have
                slashed at the shadows in vain


they come to a strand belched up by
          a stinking whirlpool      waters served by
                Charon
                        who moves
          souls across
                on a gloomy skiff
          now ancient     white-haired and wild-eyed but with
          godhead still green in his bones


The whole sorry-assed crowd bum-rushes him


mothers                 heroes           boys
          unmarried     virgins          youths dead
                before their time


like foliage swept up in the autumn wind
                or
sea birds flocking the land in winter chill


they stand
          begging for passage      but
                the old seaman takes
          now these      now those
          confining others to the banks
Aeneas
          dumbfounded at the hubbub says
"Tell me maiden why
this mob wants to cross the river?

                          or
how does he decide these get to go
while those have to stay behind?"

The aged Sibyl replies:

"Anchises' son, divine offspring,
            what you see here is hell's own marsh
            and the Stygian swamp whose power
            gives even gods pause in breaking
                        their oaths
            These souls are
            the helpless unburied hoi-polloi
                        the ferryman is Charon
            he's not allowed to take souls
            across the roaring river unless
            their bones are laid to rest.
            For a hundred years they wander
            crowding the riverbank
            until they're finally admitted
            and see the other shore."

Aeneas stands there feeling sorry for them.

# Esther Jansma

## translated by Andrew Houwen

### A Perfect Movement

It's all water it's seeing nothing
to the end of the landscape here

drowned the place where you lived
turned corners in the familiar

knowing of a body where school is
your bike goes your house stands in the small

warm places of your life the cradle rests.
It's water on which the sun crashes.

Who will know if far below
the light breaks so briefly that it seems

as if a little hand loosens itself
from what is missing or the shape of a cheek

or smaller an eyelid a glimpse of
what goes with seeing something new, wanting

to understand it? It's water, it's a fraction
of it, it's just rowing and rowing

and wishing you knew the shimmering light
in your eyes sometimes appears in the depths

as if for a moment a perfect movement
emerges there showing nothing has gone.

## Under Water

say you were totally lost gone under
water sunk not knowing the way where
there are no roads and later also forgotten

while something else in the form of languid
see-through membranes came about with toes
and fingers and eyes that got covered forever

and the grasping began while the disappearing
just carried on against or between what somewhere
far away still brought to mind rooms

in what once must have been houses
now with soft evasive swaying walls
where if you just search and feel thoroughly

even under the slimy muddied floors
there must be a place to lie down like a shrimp
in the cavity of the absence in you

to endure to think shut the familiar
wide-open staring of invisible
imperceptible holes in the blind

darkness full of water to sleep
in nothing from which nothing will emerge

## The Trying

He walks across a lawn, bends down, grabs a stick
walks to a tree and throws the stick between the branches.

The stick falls. He goes towards it, picks it up, walks
back and throws the stick between the branches. Leaves

fall down with the stick. He walks over the grass, grabs
the stick again, walks to the tree, looks up

measures the distance to the small plane stuck there
throws the stick, begins to walk to where the stick will fall

falls, stands up, grabs the stick, walks to the tree and looks
up at the place where he is a wreck in the light

and dark green not replying between the branches.

# Francis Ponge

*translated by Ian Brinton*

## Blackberries

Inside the verbal complex that is a poem, set down on the line between 'mind' and 'thing', there are certain fruits made up of separate spheres and each containing a black drop within.

Appearing in khaki, a light red, and black, rather than giving the picker 'the come-on', they suggest the separate stages of a rambling family.
With so much more seed than pulp the birds don't much care for them since there's not a lot left as they travel between beak and anus.

But during the process of the poet's constitutional he addresses this seed in his mind as follows: a great number of the flowers' patient efforts find success, knotted, within the spiky brambles. Amongst its few properties my poem is buried in the berry.

## Moss

Vegetation on reconnaissance used to halt on block-still rock. Cudgels of velvet and silk ranked there cross-legged.
Since that time, since the twitching of those lancers camped on rock, there has been a universal loss of head by those trapped and stamped and stifled.

And then the hair started growing and the world grew darker.

Self-absorbed in this growth the hair grew longer to form thick-pile carpets that bow beneath you before rising again entangled: suffocating... drowning.

Stop! Slice the razor through this spongy tissue, this saturation, these soggy mats. Re-discover ancient rock bottom.

## The Crate

Halfway along the path between a coop and a cell the French language gives us a crate, a slatted spaced container for conveying those fruits in danger of being stifled by the least hint of suffocation. Constructed for its purpose with delicacy it can be smashed up with ease and is used only once: it lasts less time than the fragile contents it holds.

On every street corner, round by the market, these boxes of balsa are stacked shining. Still so new, and a little stunned to find itself thrown off balance on its way to the tip, this object inspires a moment's sympathy without compelling us to dwell on its fate too long as we pass.

## The Lemeunier Restaurant
(Rue de la Chaussée d'Antin)

Few things more stirring than the scene before you in the enormous restaurant in the Rue de la Chaussée d'Antin: Lemeunier's where office-workers and shop-assistants take their lunch-time meal.

The magical world of bevelled mirrors and gilt ornament is dished up to the eye alongside the over-the-top lights and music. One enters this world via a dark passage, lined with pots of plants interspersed with a few early diners already in place, to emerge in a vast room with a wooden balcony running round and to be hit by a wave of warm air, the clattering clash of plates and utensils, the calls of the waitresses and the walls of hubbub.

In its enormous range of focus this is a canvas worthy of Veronese but completed in the style of Manet's famous Bar.

A little orchestra of musicians grouped on the balcony takes pride of place without any doubt; next come the cashiers hoisted up behind their counters with their bright blouses puffed out to full view; lastly the head-waiters, dapper little manikins, who move around slowly although they also, upon occasion, burst into action like the waitresses, not on account of any flash of impatience from the diners (more accustomed to being passive) but propelled by a sense of their own professional qualities which are kept up to the mark by the state of play in the job market.

O how the world of the vapid and trifling reaches its zenith here! Ranks of empty-headed young people impersonate on a daily basis the world that the genuine bourgeois allow themselves to indulge in, eight or ten times a year, on the occasion of a banker-father or a light-fingered mother catching an unexpected windfall and wishing to impress the neighbours.

Dolled up like the country cousins in Sunday best the young office-workers and their floozies throw themselves into this indulgence every day of the week. Each one clutches his plate like the hermit-crab his shell while wave upon wave of the Viennese waltz crashes over the clicking of plate, stimulating both heart and stomach.

Peeking into this grotto of enchantment I see the chatter and laughter without hearing the words. The young shop-floor salesman immersed in a crowd of look-alikes discloses the secret desires of his heart and confidently expects a return.

Brazen tiers of creamy desserts are served in long-stemmed acorn-cups fashioned in some metal; quickly rinsed out they almost invariably remain warm whilst still permitting those diners, who choose to have them placed before them, the fullest expression of feelings stirring inside them. For one it is his flamboyance<sup>1</sup> that has attracted a magnificently curvaceous typist to his side and for her attentions he would not think twice about committing a thousand similar costly displays; for another it is as if to bring attention to the stylish manner in which he had ordered a light first course so as to permit himself the indulgence of a sweet; for yet more it becomes a way of expressing upper-class disdain for all who are not prepared to partake of the magical show; and lastly there are those whose table-manners reveal the confident and well-bred style of being thoroughly habituated to such magnificence.

Meanwhile thousands of little white crumbs and larger red stains have been appearing on the taut and scattered tablecloths and napkins.

Before too long it is time for the cigarette lighters to make their appearance in roles defined for them by either their mechanisms or their manner of being manipulated. And at this time the ladies, lifting their arms to fiddle with their lipstick and pat their hairdos, reveal in different ways their little cockades of perspiration.

Now the time has arrived, in a crashing of chairs pushed back, a whiplash of dishcloths and crusty remnants, for the final act in this extraordinary display. Each in turn, the waitresses, whose apron pockets hold a notepad and in whose hair nestles a pencil, puff out their tummies, held in by their apron strings, towards their customers and quickly tot up the damage. Now is the moment for extravagance to be penalised and modesty rewarded. With coins and notes on the table being swopped to and fro everyone seems to come out a winner.

During the final acts of the evening performance, and orchestrated by the waitresses, there begins a general lifting-up of all the furniture to be concluded behind the now-closed doors. This is followed by a damp mop-up done with efficiency and brought to a smart conclusion.

It is only now that the workers, fingering the little coins deep in their pockets and thinking of a child left with the nurse in the country or staying with the neighbours, can leave the darkened premises behind without a backward glance. On the pavement opposite the men waiting for them can only see an enormous confusion of chairs and tables with their ears sticking up staring outwards in stupor at the now deserted street.

# Olga Orozco

*translated by Peter Boyle*

## Cantos to Berenice (V)

You reigned in Bubastis
your feet in earth, like the Nile,
a constellation for a headdress above your heavenly double.
You were the Sun's daughter and fought against night's malevolent
    ones –
mire, treason or mole, rodents gnawing at the house wall, at the bed
    of lovemaking –
from the bejewelled dynasties of stone
to ash-coated kitchen spices, multiplying yourself,
from the temple's halo to the steam off cooking pots.
Solitary sphinx or domestic sybil,
you were the goddess Lar and in every fold, every brushy patch
of your inexplicable anatomy, you housed a god, like some
        insomniac flea.
Through the ears of Isis or Osiris you discovered
that your names were Bastet and Bast and that other name only
        you know
(or maybe a cat doesn't need three names?)
but when the Furies nibbled away at your heart like a
        honeycomb of plagues
you puffed yourself up till you claimed kinship with the lion,
then you were called Sekhet, the revenger.
But the gods, the gods too die to be immortal
and, once again, any day they like, burn dust and garbage.
Your little bell rolled round, its music silenced by the wind.
Your little pouch lies scattered among countless mouths of sand.
And now your shield is a blurred idol for lizards and centipedes.
The centuries have bound and wrapped you in your wasted
        necropolis –
that city swathed in bandages that walks through children's
        nightmares –

91

and because each body by itself is one small part
of the immense sarcophagus of a god
you were hardly even you and, at the same time, a legion sitting
          in suspense,
seated there, you with that air
of being always at ready, sitting on guard
at the threshold.


## Cantos to Berenice (XVII)

Though all our traces may be wiped clean just like candles at dawn
and you maybe can't remember in reverse, like the White Queen,
leave me your smile in the air.
Perhaps by now you're as immense as all my dead,
with your skin night after night hiding the overflowing night of
          farewell:
one eye on Achernar, the other on Sirius,
your ears stuck to the deafening wall of other planets,
your vast body drowned in their boiling ablution,
in their Jordan of stars.
Maybe my head would be impossible, my voice not even a void,
my words less than tattered rags of some ridiculous language.
But leave me your smile in the air:
a gentle vibration to coat in quicksilver a sliver of the glass of absence,
that brief vigil tattooed in live flame in a corner,
a tender sign to perforate one by one the leaves of that harsh calendar
          of snow.
Leave me your smile
as some form of perpetual guardian,
Berenice.

## Pavane for a Dead Princess
*for Alejandra Pizarnik*

Little sentry guard,
you fall once again through the fissure of night
armed with nothing but your open eyes and terror
against the insoluble invaders of the blank page.
They were legion.
Legion made flesh was their name
and they multiplied the more you unpicked the fabric till the very last
    thread,
cowering in your corner against the voracious spiderwebs
    of nothingness.
Closing your eyes means becoming the dwelling place of the whole
    universe.
Open them and you draw the boundary line and you stay out there
    at the mercy of the sky.
To walk on that line is to lose your place.
Bouts of insomnia like long tunnels for testing every reality's
    inconsistency;
nights and more nights perforated by a single bullet that nails you into
    the dark,
the same attempt to recognise yourself on waking inside the memory
    of death:
that perverse temptation,
that adorable angel with a pig's snout.
Who spoke of spells to counteract the wound of one's own birth?
Who mentioned bribes for the emissaries of one's own future?
Only there was a garden: in the depths of everything there is a garden
where the blue flower from Novalis' dream opens.
Cruel flower, vampire flower,
more treacherous than the trap hidden in the plush of the wall,
a flower you can never reach without leaving your head or whatever
    blood you still have on the threshold.
But, not caring, you kept leaning over to pick it, with no foothold,
just inward abysses.
You planned to swap it for the starving creature who was taking over
    your house.

You built little ravenous castles in her honour;
you wore feathers that had broken free from the bonfire of every
          possible paradise;
you trained small dangerous animals to gnaw away the bridges of
          salvation;
you lost yourself just like the beggar woman with her delusion of
          wolves;
you tried out languages like acids, like tentacles,
like ropes in the hands of a strangler.
Ah what poetry does, cutting your veins with dawn's sharp edge,
and those bloodless lips sucking down venoms as speech turns empty.
And suddenly there's no more.
The flasks have shattered.
Lights and pencils cracked in splinters.
The paper was torn apart with a tear down which you glide into one
          more labyrinth.
All the doors are for getting out.
And everything is at the back of mirrors.
Little traveller,
alone with your collection box of visions
and the same unbearable sense of abandonment under your feet:
clearly with your voices you're calling out like a drowned woman for
          passage across;
clearly your enormous shadow that goes on flying above you in the
          search for another still holds you back,
or you meet an insect whose membranes hide all chaos and you tremble,
or you're frightened by the sea that, so you think, fits into this
          single tear.
But now that the silence has wrapped you twice over in its wings like
          a mantle
I tell you again:
in the depths of everything there is a garden.
Your garden is there.
Talitha cumi.

# Jacqueline Risset

*translated by Kevin Nolan*

## The War

IN THE DISTANCE

the war
the war of beginning

popoli umani   chiusi

(peoples  beings  corralled )

simili alle razze dei cavalli

(like  horse-breeds)

lontani nei pascoli lontani

(far off  in distant pastures)

war and philosophy


destroying  means
to open an ear

aged tympanum
philosophy

unknowable zoning
of light and shade

## A.R.

we are always leaving for Aden
we need to find horses, muster wagons
we make a few sorties
on fine mules with fancy bridles
but we have to make shift
grab the paperwork,
write letters,
Move it—they're waiting, pack up and go


—why did they let him sleep on?
—why didn't they help him get dressed?



## THE ENEMY

Youth—tempestuousness
  all that
      has made
         red bright fruit

so I've hefted
  a shovel
because we need
        to dig

—And who knew how
  laboured
    —strength could be ?

Eat
  and  the darkness—
    of  blood—

96

baying /
of  dogs /
darting /
of hares /
and screech /
I think /

of  one    I am /
saying to myself;
mercy!  /
so wild /

leave it /

in terror then /
I hold on /

with the force of a stone
winepress crushing eggs

in city as in forest

they have no way

to figure out the enemy
first eaten
then killed
then kept a slave

the prince,  always out hunting

no limit
to the use of ultimate force
watching the rules of the game
            quit the game?
disenchantment
insufferable

now  and everywhere
deathless un-rest

# Jordi Doce

*translated by Lawrence Schimel*

## The End of March

The indolence of the air on the rooftop
and the lukewarm roughness of the geraniums
on the neighbouring balcony–
their trembling is enough for me to know, again,
the day's simple decline,
the tenacious half-light that always returns
and seeks shelter within these lines.

Swollen and promiscuous,
the mid-afternoon sun
crashes against the façade and breaks in two:
above, into a palpable triangle,
the dense juice of the final light;
below, between flowerpots and dirty skylights,
the persistent dampness of the shadowed patio.

The light is always a higher order,
what exhumes and reveals,
what cleans and redeems,
the obligatory emblem of all transcendence.
Only at the feet of the sun or divinity
do we take on body, are we what we are,
a handful of shadow shaped by desire.

Outside, among the geraniums of the balcony,
two pigeons preside over the vespertine stillness
with greedy, ignorant eyes.
From time to time, one tilts its head
and the sun lights its crest with sudden, undeserved brilliance,
and it is as if the hand, despite everything, could hold it,
perhaps, by just opening.

## On the Rooftop

A bird that flows slowly
and, in the background, the city,
terraced and stiff
like the sea bottom.

Everything is blue to the touch–
and wakens us.

*

Clothing waves on the line.
Against the solid blue,
the whiteness of a white shirt.

For your dry lips,
for your eyes that have slept,
a little white water,
a little blue water.

*

A jar of fresh water
is not clearer than our clear eyes.

And the wind, in our eyes,
leaves behind, almost disdainfully, its eddies,
the untouchable root of another wonder.

*

We cross the rooftop.
Between laughter and blue,
the sudden theatre of the heights:
the move we don't make moves through us.

# María do Cebreiro

*translated by Neil Anderson*

## Field

(The sound of the water didn't keep her from seeing,
but rather from thinking.)

There were five of us: my friend, the kids,
the woman. There was someone else.
They left us behind.

—You almost never give names.

—The current shifted.
On the wooden bridge,
very quietly,
the third one said:
"Come with me. Don't be scared.
Hold on to my arm."

—Were you scared of the bridge or his arm?

—His insistence,
whispered, hard
as wood.

—What was his name?
—The bridge twisted round.

The woman, on the other side,
suggested
that I hike up
the hem of my dress.

"I've already been here." He doesn't believe her.

As it splashes on the ground, the detergent
paints the sea on the stones.

—You use white paper. You don't recycle.

I think you are only capable of desire.

She's not offended. She smiles.

—You're not going to tell me I'm right?
—You don't need me to.

As she entered the river, the sound of the water blinded her.

—Were you compatible, the two of you?

—One day he asked me,
"do you sort your garbage?"

—Did you stop loving him?

—I came to understand
that sometimes he preferred
to suspect.

—He was probably scared.

—He wrote with his left hand.
She was far away.

We kept walking for a bit, I had said goodbye,
but he hadn't.

We lay down in the grass.

—One wouldn't think that you were
so sensitive to landscape.
—You know how I like
to improvise.
—Tickling, taking your clothes off,
turning away from the world.
—Changing my mind, rolling around,
playing. —Getting wet, seeing you
all together.

The river came later. Running clear.

It was one of those moments when it seems that things
give us continuity, that any old thing can
carry us on.

—I would come out on top.
—I'm sure you would.

Very slowly, daylight crept
into the room. They breathe deeply.
Saying nothing, thinking nothing,
not even the air separates us.

# Notes on Contributors

TIM ALLEN now lives near Preston. Shearsman published *Settings* (2008) and *The Voice Thrower* (2011). Recent books: *The Carousing Duck* (zimZalla 2013), *Copyright* (Department 2013), *Tattered by Magnets* (Knives Forks and Spoons 2014) and *Default Soul* (Red Ceilings 2014). The poems here are from *A New Geography of Romanticism* which is due from Red Ceilings later this year.

NEIL ANDERSON is currently Visiting Assistant Professor of Spanish at Texas Tech University in Lubbock, Texas, and has a Ph.D. in Galician literature from the University of North Carolina, Chapel Hill.

JAMES BELL has published two poetry collections, *the just vanished place* (2008) and *fishing for beginners* (2010), both from tall-lighthouse. He lives in Brittany where he contributes articles to an English language journal and continues to publish poems nationally and internationally. His latest eBook is *By Shinkansen to the Deep South* (Poetry Super Highway 2013).

PETER BOYLE lives in Sydney. His most recent collection is a new and selected poems, *Towns in the Great Desert*, from Puncher & Wattman. His translation of José Kozer's *Tokonoma* was published by Shearsman in 2014.

IAN BRINTON lives in Kent and is reviews editor for *Tears in the Fence*. His translations of Yves Bonnefoy have appeared in an Oystercatcher Press chapbook and elsewhere. His has edited several volumes for Shearsman, including essays on J.H. Prynne and Peter Hughes, as well as the selected essays of Andrew Crozier. His edition of Andrew Crozier's *'Free Verse' as Formal Restraint* will be published by Shearsman in 2015.

SEAN BURN, poet and playwright, lives in Newcastle upon Tyne. His Shearsman collection, *is that a bruise or a tattoo?*, appeared in 2013.

JAMES BYRNE is editor of *The Wolf*, and teaches at Edge Hill University. He has published two collections, most recently *Blood/Sugar* (Arc, 2009). A third is forthcoming from Tupelo Press in the USA. Books he has edited/co-edited include: *The Wolf: A Decade (Poems 2002-2012)*, *Voice Recognition: 21 Poets for the 21st Century* (Bloodaxe, 2009), *Bones Will Crow: 15 Contemporary Burmese Poets* (Arc, 2012).

MICHELLE CAHILL lives in New South Wales. She edits *Mascara*, an online journal of poetry and prose. Her collection *Vishvarapa* was shortlisted in the Victorian Premier's Literary Awards and her work has been widely anthologised. The poems here are from her manuscript, *The Herring Lass*.

MARÍA DO CEBREIRO is a Galician poet, whose collection *I am not from here* was published by Shearsman in translation by Helena Miguélez-Carballeira in 2010. Her latest Galician collection is *Os inocentes* (Editorial

Galaxia, 2014). The poem here is reprinted from the previous issue as that version contained some significant typesetting errors.

**GERALDINE CLARKSON**'s poems have appeared in a variety of journals and anthologies, most recently *Ambit*, *Poetry London*, and Salt's *Best British Poetry 2014*, which features a poem first published in *j* 99 & 100. She lives in Warwickshire and is currently working towards her first collection. Note: In 'Mother's Rue' Some lines have been taken from *Songs My Mother Taught Me* by Marlon Brando).

**MARTYN CRUCEFIX**'s chapbook, *The Time We Turned*, appeared from Shearsman in 2014. Worple Press has also recently published his collection, *A Hatfield Mass*. He has five full-length collections, most recently *Hurt*, from Enitharmon. He has also translated Rilke's *Duino Elegies* and *Sonnets to Orpheus*.

**JORDI DOCE** (Gijón, 1967) is a poet, critic, and translator. He holds a Ph.D. from the University of Sheffield, and has taught both there and at Oxford. He is the author of several poetry collections, including *La anatomia del miedo*, *Otras lunas* (winner of the XXVIII City of Burgos Poetry Prize) and *Gran angular*. He has translated into Spanish books of poetry by William Blake, T. S. Eliot, Ted Hughes, Charles Simic, Charles Tomlinson, Paul Auster, Anne Carson, and many others. He lives in Madrid.

**LAURA ELLIOTT** graduated from the Norwich School of Art and Design and completed her poetry MA at UEA in 2012. Her work has featured in anthologies such as *Dear World and Everyone in It* (Bloodaxe Books) and *Best British Poetry* (Salt Publishing), as well as various print and online journals. She co-edits *Lighthouse* literary journal and lives in London.

**MICHAEL FARRELL** lives in Melbourne; his most recent collection, *Open Sesame*, was published in Sydney by Giramondo in 2012. He recently won *Australian Book Review*'s Peter Porter Poetry Prize.

**KERI FINLAYSON** has a collection from Shearsman titled *Rooms* (2009). She lives in Norfolk.

**DAVID HADBAWNIK**'s translation of Books 1-6 of the *Aeneid* will appear in an illustrated edition from Shearsman in September 2015. In 2011, he edited Jack Spicer's *Beowulf* for the CUNY Lost and Found Document series (with Sean Reynolds), and published *Field Work* (BlazeVOX Books). He is the editor and publisher of Habenicht Press and the journal *kadar koli*. He blogs at Primitive Information and lives in Buffalo, NY.

**KIRAN MILLWOOD HARGRAVE** lives in Oxford. Her work has appeared in numerous journals and magazines including *Magma*, *Orbis*, *The New Writer*, *Agenda* and *Room*, and has also been anthologised in *Catechism: Poems for Pussy Riot* (English PEN, 2012), *Sentinel Literary Anthology* (2012), *Furies* (For Books' Sake, 2014), *Wenlock Poetry Anthology* (2014) and *Raving Beauties* (Bloodaxe Books, 2015).

**Tania Hershman** lives in Bristol and is the author of the short-story collections, *The White Road and Other Stories* (Salt, 2008) and *My Mother Was an Upright Piano: Fictions* (Tangent Books, 2012). She is currently working on a PhD at Bath Spa University, and is Royal Literary Fund Writing Fellow in the faculties of science at Bristol University.

**Andrew Houwen** lives in Berkshire. His translations of Esther Jansma were read with the author at the Reading Poetry Festival in 2013 and a selection of these appeared in *Modern Poetry in Translation* in 2015. He is currently collaborating with Chikako Nihei on translations of modern Japanese poetry.

**Sarah James'** most recent poetry collection is *Be[yond]* (Knives, Forks and Spoons Press). The same publisher will issue *The Magnetic Diaries* shortly.

**Esther Jansma** is an archaeologist and one of the leading contemporary poets in the Netherlands. Her collected poetry appeared in 2006 as *Altijd Vandaag* (Always Today). Bloodaxe Books published a volume of her work in Francis R. Jones' translation in 2008,under the title *What It Is*.

**Rupert M Loydell** teaches at Falmouth University. He has several books from Shearsman, most recently *Ballads of the Alone* (2013) and *The Return of the Man Who Has Everything* (2015).

**James McLaughlin** lives in Dumbarton and has appeared in the magazine in several occasions. He has three publications from Knives Forks and Spoons Press, including *Justified Sonnets*.

**Kate Miller's** first full collection, *The Observances*, is published by Oxford Poets/Carcanet in April 2015. In 2012 she completed her Ph.D. while teaching poetry courses in the English department at Goldsmiths, University of London. She was awarded the Edwin Morgan International Poetry Prize in 2008 and has received several other awards.

**Kevin Nolan's** publications include *Alar* (Equipage) and *Loving Little Orlick* (Barque Press).

**Olga Orozco** (1920-1999) was a major Argentine poet of the 20th century. She was a member of so-called *Tercera Vanguardia*—the Third Avant-Garde—which was influenced by surrealism.

**Simon Perchik** lives on Long Island, NY. His work has been appearing in this magazine since its very first issue in 1981. His many publications include a collected poems, *Hands Collected. The Books of Simon Perchik. Poems 1949-1999* (Columbus, OH: Pavement Saw Press, 2000).

**John Phillips** lives in St Ives, Cornwall. His publications include *Language Is* (Sardines Press, San Francisco, 2005) and *What Shape Sound* (Skysill Press, Nottingham, 2011). He publishes poetry pamphlets under the imprint of Hassle Press.

FRANCIS PONGE (1899-1988) was a major 20th-century French poet and essayist. Best-known for his prose-poetry, his works include *Le savon* (*Soap*, 1969) and *Le parti pris des choses* (*The Voice of Things*, 1949).

JACQUELINE RISSET (1936-2014) was one of the major figures of postwar French literature: a master poet and critic, her work includes studies of Proust, Dante and Maurice Scève; she was also one of the founding editors of *Tel Quel*. She published seven volumes of poetry: the translations printed here are from the section entitled *The War* from her book, *Sept passages de le vie d'une femme* (Flammarion, 1985).

ALEXANDRA SASHE lives in Vienna. Shearsman published her first collection, *Antibodies*, in 2013.

LAWRENCE SCHIMEL is a New Yorker who writes in both Spanish and English and has published over a hundred books in many different genres, for both adults and children. He is the author of one poetry collection in Spanish, *Desayuno en la cama*, and two poetry chapbooks in English, *Fairy Tales for Writers* and *Deleted Names*. He has won the Lambda Literary Award twice, for his anthologies *PoMoSexuals* and *First Person Queen*. He is the publisher of the independent poetry press A Midsummer Night's Press (www.amidsummernightspress.com). He lives in Madrid, Spain where he works as a Spanish->English translator.

ROBERT SHEPPARD has a number of books from Shearsman, including *Berlin Bursts* (2011) and *A Translated Man* (2013), to be joined by a *Selected Poems* later this year. His *Complete Twentieth Century Blues* is still available from Salt Publishing.

ZOË SKOULDING was for some years editor of *Poetry Wales*, and is the author of three collections from Seren, most recently, *The Museum of Disappearing Sounds* (2013). She is a member of the collective *Parking Non-Stop*, whose CD *Species Corridor*, combining experimental soundscape with poetry and song, was released on the German label Klangbad in 2008.

SIMON SMITH's *11781 W. Sunset Boulevard* appeared from Shearsman in 2014. A *Selected Poems* is currently in development for publication in 2016, as are his editions of the poetry of Paul Blackburn, likewise for Shearsman.

ANDREW TAYLOR's first collection, *Radio Mast Horizon*, was published by Shearsman in 2013. He teaches at Nottingham Trent University.

VIRGIL (PUBLIUS VERGILIUS MARO, 70BC-19BC) should need no introduction. His *Aeneid* was the national epic of Ancient Rome—commissioned by Emperor Augustus—although incomplete at the time of the author's death; Virgil's other major works were the *Eclogues* and the *Georgics*.

www.ingramcontent.com/pod-product-compliance
Lightning Source LLC
Chambersburg PA
CBHW030957090426
42737CB00007B/576